MONTANA

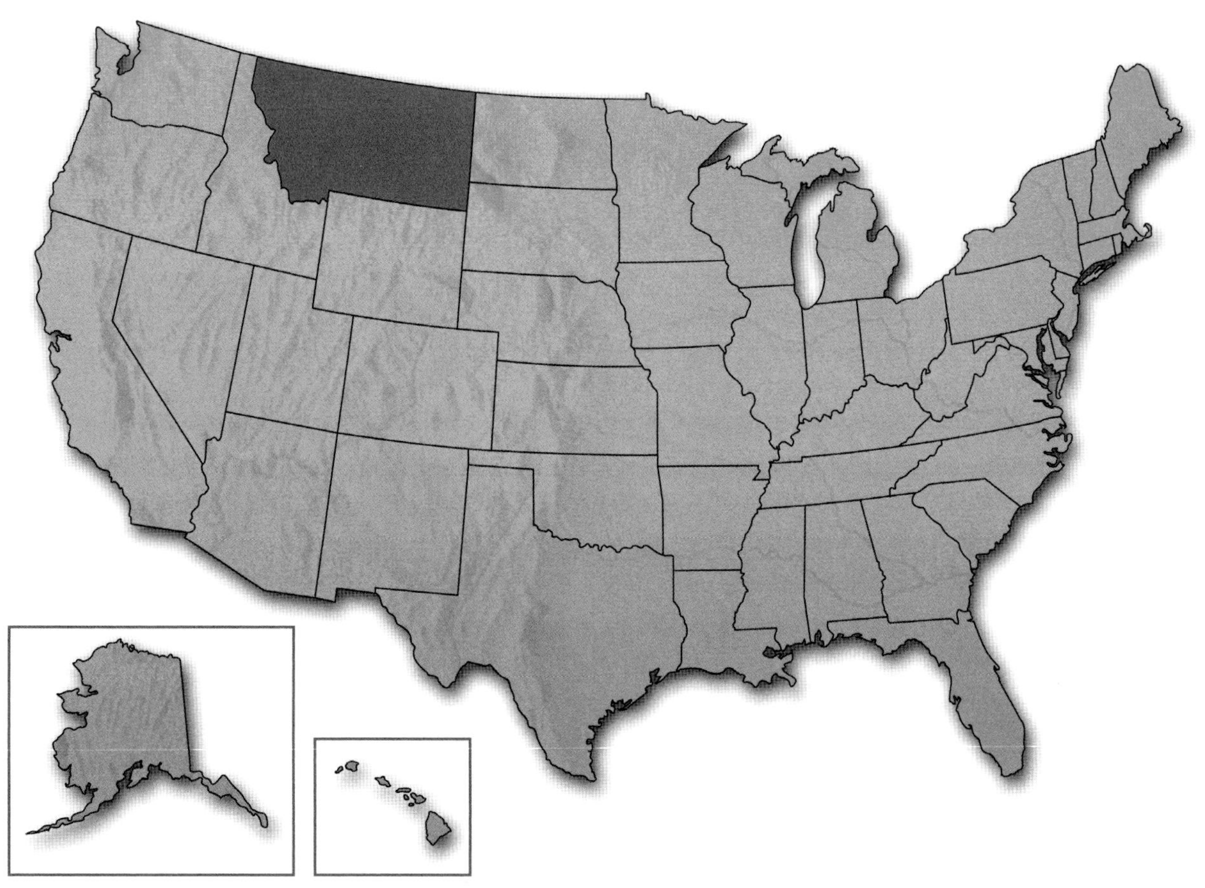

Krista McLuskey

Published by Weigl Publishers Inc.
123 South Broad Street, Box 227
Mankato, MN 56002
USA
Web site: http://www.weigl.com

Library of Congress Cataloging-in-Publication Data

McLuskey, Krista, 1974-
Montana / Krista McLuskey.
p. cm. -- (A kid's guide to American states)
Includes index.
ISBN 1-930954-92-1 (lib. bdg.)
1. Montana--Juvenile literature. [1. Montana.] I. Title. II. Series.

F731.3 .M38 2001
2001017997

ISBN 1-930954-83-2 (pbk.)

Printed in the United States of America
1 2 3 4 5 6 7 8 9 10 05 04 03 02 01

Project Coordinator
Jennifer Nault
Substantive Editor
Leslie Strudwick
Copy Editor
Heather Kissock
Designers
Warren Clark
Terry Paulhus
Photo Researcher
Angela Lowen

Photograph Credits

Every reasonable effort has been made to trace ownership and to obtain permission to reprint copyright material. The publishers would be pleased to have any errors or omissions brought to their attention so that they may be corrected in subsequent printings.

Cover: Grizzly Bears (Corel Corporation), Rocky Mountains (Corel Corporation) **Archive Photos:** page 25BR; **Eric R. Berndt/The Image Finders:** pages 9T, 14BL; **Bettmann/CORBIS:** page 21T, 27T; **Janet Cobb/The Image Finders:** page 22T; **Corel Corporation:** pages 3M, 6BL, 10BR, 11T, 11B, 13B, 29T, 29B; **Denver Public Library:** pages 16T, 16B, 17T, 17BR, 18ML, 18BR, 19T, 19B; **Owen Franken/CORBIS:** page 14BR; **Mark E. Gibson/The Image Finders:** page 23BR; **Jeff Greenberg/The Image Finders:** page 22B; **Robbie Jack/CORBIS:** page 24BR; **Wolfgang Kaehler/CORBIS:** page 9BR; **Lampo Communications:** page 14T; **Buddy Mays/CORBIS:** page 20BR; **New York Times Co./Archive Photos:** page 21BL; **PhotoDisc Corporation:** pages 15T, 15BR, 20T; **Photofest:** page 25BL; **Travel Montana:** pages 4TL, 4BL, 12BL, 13T, 25T, 28T; **Travel Montana/D Broussard:** page 17BL; **Travel Montana/Craig & Liz Larcom:** page 28B; **Travel Montana/Donnie Sexton:** pages 3T, 3B, 4BR, 5T, 6T, 6BR, 7T, 7B, 8T, 8B, 9BL, 10BL, 12T, 12BR, 18T, 21BR, 23T, 24BL, 26T, 26BL, 27B; **Travel Montana/S. Shimek:** page 20ML; **Travel Montana/M Van Donsel:** page 10T; **Travel Montana/G Wunderwald:** page 5ML; **Tutsky Group:** page 24T; **University of Montana:** page 26BR.

CONTENTS

There are more than 22 million acres of forest in Montana.

INTRODUCTION

When explorers Meriwether Lewis and William Clark first entered Montana, they were awestruck by the large, open plains and the number of animals roaming the land. Today, much of the Montana landscape that Lewis and Clark crossed remains unchanged. From river canyons and mountain meadows to the Great Plains, Montana has kept much of its natural beauty intact.

Wild forests, rugged mountain terrain, and rivers abundant in fish are just some of the reasons Montana is considered to be "The Last Best Place." The lack of big cities with noise, pollution, and crowds also fosters this view. In fact, there are fewer people in the whole state of Montana than there are in many cities in the United States. Skyscrapers are scarce, and many people live on acreages or farms. Montana has earned the reputation as one of the few remaining retreats from the hectic pace of big city life.

QUICK FACTS

Montana is officially nicknamed "The Treasure State" for its wealth of mineral resources.

The word *Montana* means "mountainous" in Spanish.

Montana is the fourth-largest state in the nation, with an area of 147,046 square miles. Only Alaska, Texas, and California are larger.

Miles City bears the nickname, "The Cowboy Capital of the World."

The state motto is *Oro y Plata*, which means "gold and silver" in Spanish.

Cattle drives provide the opportunity to relive Montana's frontier past.

Montana has approximately 69,890 miles of highways.

Getting There

Idaho, Wyoming, North Dakota, and South Dakota all border Montana. Three Canadian provinces, Alberta, British Columbia, and Saskatchewan, border the state to the north. Montana is easily reached in this modern era of interstates and airplanes. Still, people traveling by automobile are often shocked at the size of the state. The highways seem endless, stretching as far as the eye can see. The state's road conditions can change in a flash—it can be dry one moment and icy the next. In the winter, interstates sometimes close due to heavy snow.

Air travel is available to those leaving and entering the state. The Billings Logan International Airport has almost 700,000 passenger departures and arrivals each year. It is considered to be one of the largest and busiest airports in the northern Rockies.

QUICK FACTS

The state bird is the western meadowlark.

Montana's state flower, the bitterroot, can live for a year without water.

At 200 square miles, Flathead Lake is the largest natural lake in the western United States.

Granite Peak is Montana's highest mountain at 12,799 feet. Some adventurous climbers use the Froze-to-Death Plateau route. This route is known for its many storms.

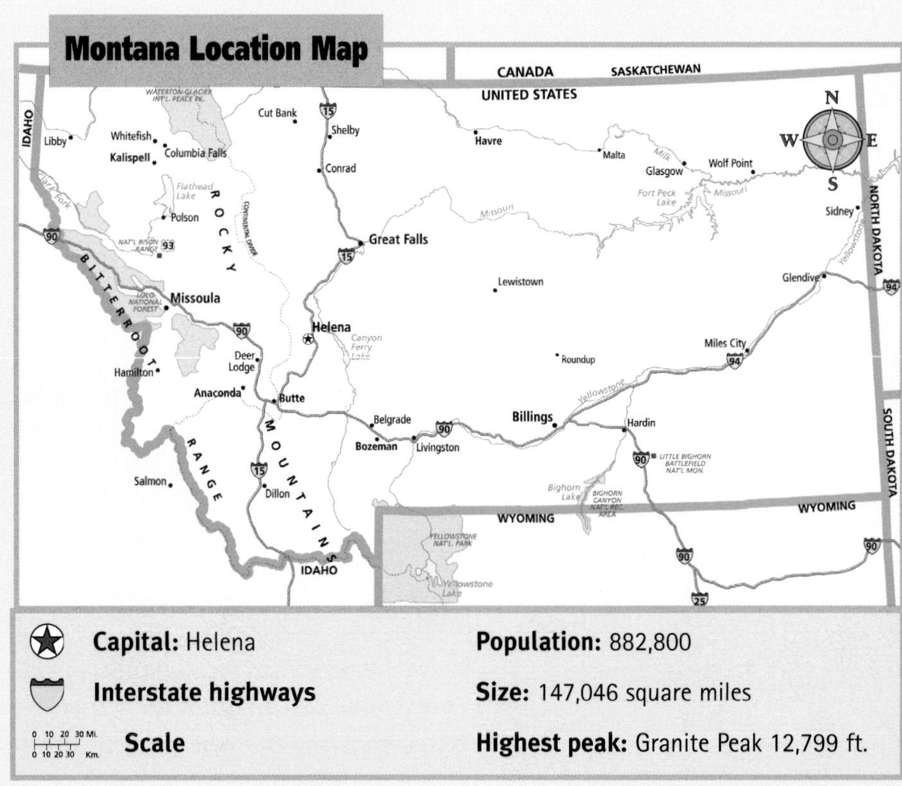

The Smokejumper Visitor Center in Missoula is the largest smokejumper base in the United States.

Montana's natural areas are sometimes threatened by blazing forest fires. Forest fires destroy many acres of land in the state every year. In 1988, flames burned a third of Yellowstone National Park. In the summer of 2000, fires turned a staggering 1 million acres of Montana's forest into ash.

Montanans have gained much recognition for combatting these fires with creativity and determination. The state leads the nation in the training of smokejumpers. These specially trained firefighters parachute into remote areas that vehicles cannot reach. Once they reach the ground, smokejumpers tackle the flames at close range. When the fires have been extinguished, there is often more work to do. Many people in the state pitch in to help those affected by disaster.

QUICK FACTS

Norman Maclean, a popular author from Montana, wrote about Montana's smokejumpers and the horrible Mann Gulch fire in his novel, *Young Men and Fire*.

There are 250 lakes in Montana's Glacier National Park.

The Maiasaur, which was a duck-billed dinosaur, is Montana's state fossil. Maiasaurs are believed to have taken great care of their young, and their name means "good mother lizard."

Forest fires can be good for the environment. They eliminate dead trees, allowing the sun to reach shorter trees.

With its high mountain peaks, forests, prairies, and valleys, the Montana landscape is beautiful and diverse.

With such a large amount of space, it should come as no surprise that many Montanans depend on the land for their livelihood. These Montanans are farmers, ranchers, or loggers. Most Montanans also cherish the land for what it offers in terms of recreation. People who love the outdoors can hike, camp, fish, and ski in the natural beauty of the state. In fact, many people move to Montana to pursue outdoor activities, such as fly fishing, downhill skiing, and snowboarding. It is no coincidence that some members of the U.S. Snowboard Team live in Montana year round.

A deep appreciation of the land has prompted many Montanans to protect the environment. To reduce automobile pollution, some cities offer free access to bikes. **Environmentalists** also pursue ways to keep the water clean and the wilderness free from development. Montanans work hard to protect the land.

QUICK FACTS

Montana's largest artificial lake is 83 square miles. Fort Peck Lake was created when the Missouri River was dammed. It has 1,520 miles of shoreline.

The longest river in the United States begins where Montana's Gallatin, Madison, and Jefferson rivers meet. The Missouri River flows 2,540 miles across the United States. It eventually flows into the Mississippi River in Missouri.

Meriwether Lewis and William Clark stumbled upon evidence of Montana's state tree, the ponderosa pine, before they even entered the area. They found pine cones that were carried by the Missouri river.

Custer National Forest in Montana provides some of the best hiking in the state.

Montana's January temperatures range from 20° Fahrenheit to 14°F.

LAND AND CLIMATE

Montana has two distinct land regions. The Great Plains are to the east, and the Rocky Mountains are to the west. The Great Plains offer mostly treeless, rolling terrain. This two-thirds of the state is ideal for agriculture, with many wheat fields sprawled across the region.

The Rocky Mountains make up the western third of the state. Mountain ranges tower over the plains in jagged rock formations. There are over fifty mountain ranges in Montana's Rocky Mountains. Snow covers some of the highest peaks about ten months of the year. Glaciers and rivers are found in these areas, too. Rivers flow toward the Kootenai and Clark Fork Rivers. Some rivers move eastward, connecting to the Yellowstone and Missouri Rivers.

QUICK FACTS

The highest recorded temperature in Montana was 117° F on July 20, 1893.

Montanans braced themselves against the state's lowest recorded temperature on January 20, 1954. The temperature fell to –70°F at Rogers Pass.

Western Montanans are given brief breaks from the cold of winter when a **chinook** blows into the state. Warm winds temporarily raise the temperature and melt the snow.

The Lewis and Clark Caverns, 300 feet below the earth's surface, are a popular tourist destination in Montana.

Glacier National Park covers over 1 million acres of land, and has 63 species of mammals and 272 species of birds.

Fort Peck in northeastern Montana is known to have a very pleasant spring and autumn.

NATURAL RESOURCES

Many of the trees logged for commercial use are from the western part of Montana.

One-quarter of Montana is covered in thick forests. Trees, including Douglas fir, spruce, pine, and cedar, are very important to the state's economy. They are cut down to make products such as paper, pencils, and log homes.

Early settlers were delighted to strike gold in Montana. Since then, many other precious metals, such as copper and silver, have been discovered in the state. Montana's environment became damaged from the **extraction** of these metals. In some mining sites, chemicals harmed the soil, water, and plant and animal life. In Anaconda, a mining site was found to have poisoned the land with deadly chemicals. In 1994, the Anaconda mining area became a **Superfund** site. Montana was given government aid to restore the area.

QUICK FACTS

The Great Plains of eastern Montana was swampland millions of years ago. As plants and animals died, they sank to the bottom of the swamp. Today, their remains are an important natural resource—coal.

Christmas trees are grown on tree farms in Montana. Each December they are shipped nationwide.

Montanans produce about 40 percent of their own power with hydroelectric, or water generated, plants.

Part of the job of Montana's forest rangers is to educate the public about the conservation and protection of the state's natural resources.

PLANTS AND ANIMALS

A rare and beautiful animal—the grizzly bear—inhabits the dense forests of Montana's Rocky Mountains. Montana is home to 80 percent of all the grizzly bears in the lower forty-eight states. Grizzlies move as fast as a horse, are as high as 8 feet, and can weigh more than 500 pounds. Another rare animal, the bald eagle, can be spotted soaring overhead. After almost being hunted to **extinction**, bald eagles have begun to return to the region.

Many other animals are also found in the state. Moose, mountain goats, and elk roam the land in western Montana. The grassy eastern plains are home to herds of pronghorn antelope and deer.

Montana's rivers contain a "living fossil." The paddlefish, the state's largest fish, is about 5 feet in length and 100 pounds. Incredibly, the paddlefish has remained mostly unchanged for about 300 million years.

Grizzly bears will fiercely defend their ranges, and will even fight other bears to protect their territory.

QUICK FACTS

The largest paddlefish caught in Montana was 142 pounds.

The grizzly bear's blonde-tipped hair and its shoulder hump **distinguishes** it from the black bear.

Cougars, which are hard to spot in the wild, are known as "The Ghosts of the Rockies."

The root of Montana's state flower, the bitterroot, was once eaten by Montana's Native Peoples. The Bitterroot Valley and the Bitterroot River were named after this small herb with beautiful pink flowers.

QUICK FACTS

Wolves prey on sick or weak deer, keeping the population down so the environment can support the healthy animals.

In the early 1900s, there were about 35,000 wolves in the Yellowstone **ecosystem**. By the 1930s, there were only a few wolves remaining.

Some ranchers were upset at wolf reintroduction because wolves kill not only wild animals, but also livestock. The environmental group Defenders of Wildlife came up with a plan. They funded a program that gave ranchers money for any livestock killed by wolves.

Hundreds of bird species call Montana home. Game birds in Montana include the ring-necked pheasant, chucker partridge, and many varieties of grouse.

The plant life growing among Montana's peaks and valleys differs from that of the flat plains. The mountains are covered in towering spruce, pine, and cedar trees. Wildflowers such as bluebells, asters, and brightly tinted Indian paintbrushes grow nearby. In the eastern plains, spiky prairie cacti poke up among shoots of blue grama grass and needlegrass.

Some animals in Montana have been harmed by humans. Since many people feared the wolf, this animal was almost hunted to extinction. It soon became obvious that the drastic change in wolf population was harmful to other animals in the region. Loss of the wolf was affecting the ecosystem. The government made an effort to increase the wolf population in Montana. In 1995, gray wolves were **reintroduced** to Yellowstone National Park.

Fourteen gray wolves were introduced to Yellowstone National Park in 1995, and another seventeen in 1996. Since then, more than eighty pups have been born in the park.

Partly because of its low population, Montana has some of the least crowded ski resorts in North America.

TOURISM

It is Montana's wide-open spaces, remote mountain pathways, and snow-covered slopes that draw people to the state. The scenic mountain region provides challenging ski slopes in the winter and wonderful hiking and horseback riding paths in the summer. In the summer, tourists can put on a cowboy hat and take in one of the state's many rodeos. More than 6 million tourists visit Montana each year. The many tourists that vacation in Montana provide employment for about 25,000 residents.

Montana's state and national parks also draw many visitors to the state. There are eighty-nine state parks, recreation areas, and monuments in Montana. Yellowstone National Park is always a major tourist attraction. Another big attraction is Glacier National Park on Montana's northern border. On the other side of the border is Canada's Waterton National Park. The two parks merged in 1932 to create the Waterton-Glacier International Peace Park.

QUICK FACTS

In 1999, tourists spent $1.6 billion in Montana.

Yellowstone National Park lies mostly in Wyoming. However, three of the park entrances are located in southern Montana.

Over one-third of the land in Montana is owned by the government.

Glacier National Park has fifty small glaciers.

Glacier National Park has more than 700 miles of beautiful hiking trails. While hiking, it is not uncommon to come across a surefooted mountain goat. These animals mostly live among rugged mountain peaks and above the timberline.

Cropland in Montana accounts for about 19 percent of the state's total area.

INDUSTRY

Montana's economy is largely based on agriculture, including ranching. There are three times as many cows in the state as there are people. The 2.7 million cows in Montana provide milk and beef. There are also about 370,000 sheep in the state. In addition to milk and meat, the sheep provide wool, which is spun into items such as sweaters and blankets. Ostrich and emu farms have recently begun to pop up across the state, starting a new ranching trend.

Agriculture in Montana is also largely based on crops. There are almost 30,000 farms covering 57.5 million acres of land. Remarkably, Montana ranks fourth in the nation for wheat production. Other crops grown in Montana include barley, sugar beets, sunflowers, and mint.

There is a large forestry industry in Montana. A great challenge, however, has been finding a balance between logging companies, which employ many people, and protecting the land for future generations. The government has protected some of Montana's forests from logging. Still, more than two-thirds of the state's forests are eligible for logging.

QUICK FACTS

Montana's mining industry is strong. Coal, petroleum, and natural gas are all important to the state's economy.

About 8 million pounds of honey is produced in Montana each year.

One cow can eat up to 24 pounds of hay per day.

Cows graze from 8–12 hours per day.

Products with the label "Made in Montana" include coffee, candy, jams, and honey.

GOODS AND SERVICES

In stores across the state, many products proudly display a "Made in Montana" sticker. The Made in Montana program was created in 1984. Its main goal is to help Montanans succeed in business. Products that have been crafted or grown and prepared in Montana bear this seal. Buyers of these products know that they are supporting local businesses and buying quality goods.

From jams to gems, Montana produces many goods. The state is famous for its juicy chokecherries, plums, and huckleberries. Most are enjoyed in the form of jams, preserves, jellies, and syrups. Precious Yogo sapphires are found in western Montana. These gems are crafted into fine jewelry and sold nationwide. Copper, an important natural resource in the state, is used in many items. Copper bracelets, belt buckles, and cookware are all crafted in Montana.

QUICK FACTS

The state gemstones are the agate and the sapphire.

There are many vegetable and fruit canneries in the Bitterroot Valley.

Most of the log homes that are manufactured in Montana are shipped to Japan.

Products made from copper can be found in stores throughout Montana.

QUICK FACTS

There are almost 100 elk and deer farms in the state of Montana.

Hunting is a popular activity in the state. Many Montanans make their living as hunting guides.

Montana is increasing its manufacturing of high-technology goods. Laser products used in dentistry, environmental cleanup, and underwater imaging are produced in the state. Many companies find Montana's highly skilled and educated workers to be a good reason for setting up their businesses in the state. Montana ranked fourth in the nation in funding for education in 1998. With two universities, five colleges of technology, and many private and tribal colleges, Montana's workforce is known for its high level of education.

The service industry is Montana's top industry. It brings in 75 percent of Montana's **gross state product**. Jobs in the service industry are growing at a faster pace than jobs in manufacturing. Service-related jobs include government jobs such as military workers, jobs in finance, such as bank tellers, and hotel and restaurant positions. Since Montana's land is largely government-owned, many workers are required to tend the parks and natural areas, such as park wardens.

Some of Montana's high-technology industries are involved in the research and development of lasers.

There were many Crow and Blackfeet buffalo jumps in Montana. Sometimes, the buffalo were lured to the edge of a cliff by Native Americans cloaked in animal skins.

FIRST NATIONS

Montana's early Native Peoples can be divided into two regional groups: those who lived in the Great Plains in eastern Montana, and those who lived near the Rocky Mountains. The Kootenai lived in the mountains, although extreme winter cold would force them down to the foothills every year. The Crow, Cheyenne, and Blackfoot lived on the Great Plains, and became known as the Plains Indians.

The thousands of buffalo that thundered across the plains of Montana were an important food source to early inhabitants of the area. All groups smoked and dried buffalo meat. Each part of the buffalo had a special use.

To catch the swift-moving buffalo, Native Peoples built corrals near steep cliffs and drove stampeding herds into them. They would then chase the buffalo off the edge of the cliff. These cliffs were known as buffalo jumps or *pishkun*. The buffalo carcasses at the base of the cliff were used for food, shelter, and tools.

QUICK FACTS

Evidence of a group of humans living in Montana between 9,000 BC to 8,000 BC has been found near Helena. This group is known as the Folsom.

Many of the Native Peoples that were living in Montana's western mountains fished in streams and gathered edible wild flowers and roots.

Buffalo hide was used to make most of the Native Americans' clothing, including **moccasins.**

Native Peoples crafted buffalo hides into teepees and furry blankets to keep warm during Montana's harsh winters.

The Crow were originally called *Absarokee*, which means "children of the large beaked bird" in Hidatsa.

Not only did the horse allow Native Peoples to follow the buffalo, it also gave them the speed that was required for a successful hunt.

The arrival of the horse forever changed the way Montana's Native Peoples hunted. By 1750, most groups, both in the mountains and on the plains, had horses. With horses, Native Americans no longer had to wait for buffalo to enter the area. Instead, they could follow the buffalo. On horseback, they could charge alongside their prey, killing them at close range.

By the late 1700s, the buffalo hunt was much easier. Buffalo were no longer hunted just for survival. They were also traded and sold.

The horse also changed relationships among Native-American groups. Before the introduction of the horse, the different groups rarely came into contact. The horse bridged the distance. While traveling, Native Peoples with horses could carry more food, clothing, and other **necessities**. Native Americans could easily meet for **powwows** and other special events.

QUICK FACTS

Native Americans often peeled the bark from ponderosa pines and ate the inner bark.

Thousands of Native Americans died when they came into contact with Europeans. Their bodies had never been exposed to smallpox before, so they had no defense against the virus.

Montana's Native Peoples used more than fifty kinds of local plants for medicine.

Native Americans were often depicted as the main hunters of buffalo. But European settlers also killed large numbers of buffalo—almost to the point of extinction.

In Great Falls, Montana, there is a bronze statue of Meriwether Lewis and William Clark.

EXPLORERS AND MISSIONARIES

The United States paid about $15 million to France for the Louisiana Territory in 1803. This deal, which included land from Louisiana in the southeast to Montana in the northwest, doubled the size of the United States. Montana became the property of this young country.

President Thomas Jefferson sent Meriwether Lewis and William Clark to explore the new area in 1805. Upon their return, Lewis and Clark reported that many fur-bearing animals, such as beavers, lived in Montana. This news inspired the next set of explorers to see Montana—especially fur traders and mountain men. Fort Raman became Montana's first fur-trading post less than a year after Lewis and Clark's **expedition**.

In 1840, a Jesuit missionary, Father Pierre Jean De Smet, came to Montana. The first mission, St. Mary's Mission, brought religion and new methods of agriculture to the Native Americans.

QUICK FACTS

A French trader named Toussaint Charbonneau, and his Shoshone wife, Sacajawea, helped Lewis and Clark find their way through Montana.

Sacajawea

So many beavers were trapped from 1807 to 1840 that the animal almost became extinct in Montana.

Christian missionaries were known as "Black Robes" because of their distinctive black clothing.

St. Mary's Mission was the first permanent mission in Montana.

The Battle of Little Bighorn is considered to be one of the worst military disasters in United States history.

EARLY SETTLERS

Montana's gold rush became a gold boom in 1862, when this precious metal was discovered along Grasshopper Creek. Soon after, hundreds of miners headed to Montana. Many miners soon turned to raising cattle on the open ranges as well. This was the beginning of Montana's ranching tradition.

At this time, the government moved Montana's Native Americans to **reservations**, but settlers were not content—they also wanted the reservation land to farm and mine. In 1876, Native Americans fought back. In the Battle of Little Bighorn, Native Americans, led by Sitting Bull and Crazy Horse, fought and beat Lieutenant Colonel George Custer and his soldiers. Still, by 1877, all of Montana's Native Peoples were forced onto reservations.

QUICK FACTS

Miners who were unlucky in the California gold rush tried mining in Montana. Last Chance Gulch (Helena) was the location of one of the first gold strikes in the area.

A large vein of copper was discovered in Butte Hill in the late 1800s. It became known as "The Richest Hill on Earth."

In the first 5 years that gold was discovered in Montana, more than $30 million worth of gold was removed from the area.

Since agriculture, one of Montana's main industries, uses much land, the state has a relatively low population. Montana is the sixth-least populated state in the nation.

POPULATION

Although it is the fourth largest state in terms of size, Montana's population is surprisingly low. There are fewer than 1 million people living in the state. In 1900, there were about 243,300 people living in Montana. Today, the largest city in Montana is Billings, with slightly less than 100,000 inhabitants. Only Billings and Great Falls are considered **metropolitan** areas.

The western and the southern parts of the state are the most populated in Montana. About half of Montanans live in cities, and the other half live in rural areas. On average, there are only six Montanans per square mile. The national average of persons per square mile is seventy-seven. With this much space, Montana certainly deserves the reputation as "The Last Best Place."

QUICK FACTS

Montana has about 882,800 residents.

The discovery of gold and silver was the main reason for Montana's population growth in the 1800s.

About 93 percent of Montanans are of European descent, 5 percent are Native American, and the remaining are Hispanic American, Asian American, or African American.

Billings, founded in 1882, was initially a town for Northern Pacific Railway workers.

POLITICS AND GOVERNMENT

Missoulian Jeannette Rankin was the first woman to be elected to the United States Congress. Rankin was a champion for equal rights and a suffragette.

In 1889, the constitution of the new state of Montana was written. In 1972, the constitution was updated, and it governs the state to this day.

The government in Montana has three branches—executive, legislative, and judicial. In the executive branch are the governor, lieutenant governor, secretary of state, and the attorney general. All members of this branch serve four-year terms. Montana's legislature has 50 senators and 100 representatives. Senators serve four-year terms and representatives hold office for two years. The state's courts are headed by a supreme court with seven court justices.

QUICK FACTS

Politician Mike Mansfield was born in Great Falls, Montana, in 1903.

Mike Mansfield served as the senate majority leader longer than any other person at that time. He served from 1961 to 1977.

The Capitol, in Helena, was renovated in 2000, at a cost of $26 million.

Montana's Scottish citizens celebrate their culture with Highland games, dance, and music.

CULTURAL GROUPS

Many immigrants came to western Montana to work in the silver and copper mines in the 1800s. Soon after, more newcomers made their way to the eastern plains to claim the huge amounts of land for farming. At the time, Montana had too much work for the few people available, and Europe was facing the opposite problem. People came from Ireland, Germany, Poland, and Italy to earn a living and begin a new life. Different ethnic groups settled in Montana and began their own communities.

Several religious groups also **migrated** to Montana. Mennonites settled in Montana, but many left when the government outlawed speaking German in the state during World War II. Mormons, members of the Church of Jesus Christ of Latter-day Saints, also came to Montana. They stayed, and now the Mormon religion is the fourth-largest religion in the state.

QUICK FACTS

In 1910, 25 percent of Montana's residents were from countries other than the United States.

Many Montana towns, such as Glasgow and Zurich, were named after cities in the home countries of newcomers.

There are seven Native-American reservations in Montana: Blackfeet, Fort Belknap, Rocky Boy's, Northern Cheyenne, Crow, Fort Peck, and Flathead. Eleven different tribes live on these reservations.

A great number of people from Germany moved to Montana in its early days. Today, the state has many German festivals, including *Oktoberfest*.

Every August in Montana, thousands of people come together for the Crow Fair and Powwow.

There are thirty-nine Hutterite colonies in Montana. Hutterites believe strongly in living simple, nonviolent lives. They live in small communities and avoid much of modern society. Instead of living in busy cities, Hutterites live in rural communities, or colonies, with few neighbors. Farming is an important economic activity within the colonies, and the Hutterites sell their goods in nearby cities or towns.

Although they were once Montana's sole residents, today only 5 percent of Montana's population is Native American. Many live on reservations. Reservations uphold long-standing Native American traditions. They also provide opportunities for education and training. For instance, Stone Child College at Rocky Boy's Indian Reservation offers degree programs in arts and sciences. Many reservations strike a balance between modern and traditional ways of life.

QUICK FACTS

Sixty percent of the pork produced in Montana comes from Hutterite farms. Hutterites also raise chickens, providing about 50 percent of the state's eggs.

Hutterite clothing is distinctive. Women wear scarves on their heads and long skirts. Men dress in dark trousers and wear dark hats.

The Festival of Nations takes place in Red Lodge every August. The festival is a celebration of world peace, showcasing ethnic crafts, food, and music.

The Blackfeet Indian Reservation is home to the Blackfeet Community College, which serves about 15,000 students.

Along with Montana, many Hutterites are settled in North and South Dakota, and Washington.

There are approximately 4,000 Hutterites living in colonies in Montana.

The Missoula carousel was created with the help of more than 200 volunteers.

ARTS AND ENTERTAINMENT

Children can find plenty of fun activities in Montana. Along the bank of the Clark Fork River in Missoula, an old-fashioned carousel spins under thousands of dazzling lights. It is the first fully hand-carved carousel to be built in the United States since the 1930s. Each horse on the carousel has a story behind its making. Horses are designed to honor local residents, or are based on Native-American culture.

The Missoula Children's Theatre International Tour (MCT) travels the world making children's dreams of acting come true. Every year, two MCT directors journey to cities in the United States, as well as other countries. They find fifty children and stage a musical play in just one week. Most of the plays are fairy tales and children's stories. Popular classics performed by MCT include *Cinderella* and *The Wizard of Oz*. In MCT, everyone gets a chance. Even very shy children find the courage to sing on stage in front of an audience. People are amazed at the high-quality performances put together in such a short time.

QUICK FACTS

Each horse on the Missoula carousel took volunteers 400 to 800 hours to make.

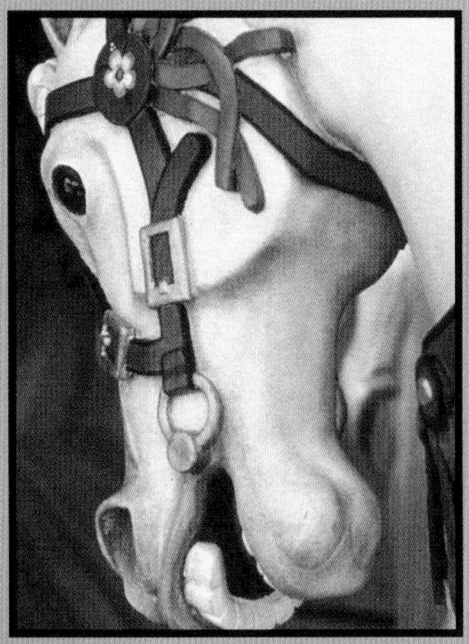

Jeff Ament, Pearl Jam's bass guitar player, brings the band to his home state of Montana to perform regularly.

World famous pianist George Winston grew up in eastern Montana. His 1999 recording, *Plains*, celebrates the region.

The Missoula Children's Theater International Tour is the largest touring children's theater in the United States.

Charlie Russell lived the life of a Montana cowboy for eleven years before gradually gaining recognition as a self-taught artist.

Some famous people have called Montana home. Young Charlie Russell had two passions—to be a cowboy and to draw wildlife. When he was 16 years old, his father sent him to Montana, and his dreams became reality. Charlie's career as an artist began in 1887. He illustrated a terrible winter in Montana by drawing a starving, frozen cow surrounded by wolves. This work of art is called *Waiting for a Chinook*. Charlie was interested in Native Americans and their rich culture, painting them in detail. He is considered to be one of the greatest painters and sculptors of the early West.

A wild stuntman hails from the Treasure State. Evel Knievel has earned the reputation as the greatest motorcycle daredevil in the world. In 1966, Evel began his career as a stuntman. He performed dangerous motorcycle jumps—flying off ramps and sailing over objects. Evel has jumped over as many as fifty cars at one time! Today, Evel Knievel's son, Robbie, performs motorcycle stunts. Just like his dad, Robbie delights and shocks fans with his amazing antics.

QUICK FACTS

A number of famous people have made Montana their home or frequent retreat. Celebrities such as journalist Connie Chung and television mogul Ted Turner head to the state.

Connie Chung

Many movies have been filmed in Montana, including *A River Runs Through It*, *The Horse Whisperer*, and *Forrest Gump*.

The first annual Montana Festival of the Book was held in September 2000. It celebrated Montana's famous writers.

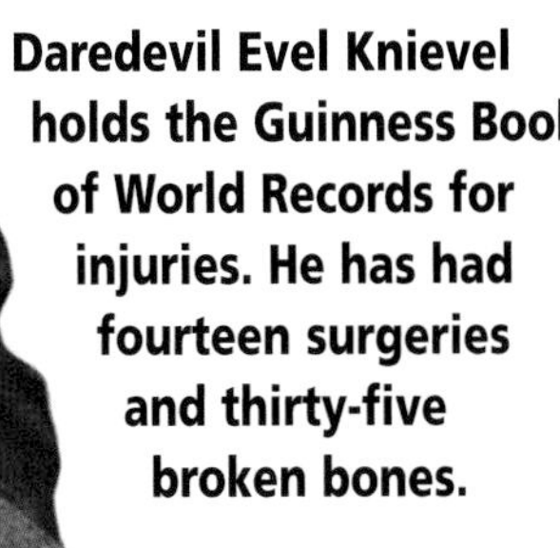

Daredevil Evel Knievel holds the Guinness Book of World Records for injuries. He has had fourteen surgeries and thirty-five broken bones.

There are thousands of miles of rivers and streams in Montana for fishers.

SPORTS

Fly-fishing is perhaps the sport most closely associated with Montana. The book and movie, *A River Runs Through It*, depicted the rivers near Missoula as a fisher's paradise. Norman Maclean, the author, wrote of his trips to the Clark Fork River with his father and brother. Today, people can be seen practicing their fly casting in many open areas. During fishing season, people from all over the country head to Montana's rivers and streams.

There are two main university teams that delight sports fans in Montana—the Bobcats and the Grizzlies. The residents of Bozeman and Missoula come out to watch these competitive matches in basketball, football, and volleyball. Signs of support are plastered throughout Missoula, home of the University of Montana Grizzlies. The scene is the same in Bozeman, the hometown of the Montana State University Bobcats.

QUICK FACTS

The University of Montana Grizzly football team won five Big Sky Conference Championships in the 1990s.

The first Wild Horse Stampede was held at the turn of the century. Today, this three-day rodeo features a competition where people saddle up and ride wild horses.

An annual rodeo held east of Helena is called the Wildest One Day Show on Earth.

Monte, the University of Montana's mascot, delights and entertains fans of all ages at sporting events.

With the state's many mountains, ice climbing is growing in popularity in Montana.

As a Rocky Mountain state with snowy winters, Montana has become a haven for winter sport enthusiasts. Some sports are extreme—they are dangerous and require great skill. Blade running is one such sport. Professional skydivers jump out of a helicopter over a ski hill. Their parachute keeps them in the air while they wind through a course of 10-foot-tall banners, called blades. Part of their bodies have to stay below the banners, but their feet cannot touch the ground.

Ice sailing and ice surfing are activities in Montana for people who enjoy speed. On special boats, wind propels winter sailors across frozen lakes at unbelievable speeds. The world record speed in ice sailing is 146 miles per hour. Ice surfers attach blades to their shoes and cling to a sail that fills with wind as they "surf" across the ice.

Another popular winter sport is downhill skiing. The state boasts sixteen downhill ski areas, with great snow and virtually no crowds. Since Montana is a large state with a small population, the lines for the ski lifts are rarely long. Snowboarders are also welcome at every one of Montana's ski areas. Many of the state's ski resorts offer remarkable snowboard parks, featuring half-pipes, board jumps, and banked turns.

QUICK FACTS

World-class ice climbers come to the Bozeman area for challenging climbs.

Hiking and camping are popular summer pastimes in Montana's mountains.

The first luge run ever built in North America was at Lolo Hot Springs in 1965.

Race to the Sky is a 350-mile dog-sled race commemorating the use of dog sleds during World War II.

Brain Teasers

1

What natural feature in Montana has earned the state a spot in the Guinness Book of World Records?

Answer: Montana's Roe River is recognized as the world's shortest river. It measures 200 feet, connecting Giant Springs and the Missouri River near Great Falls.

2

What is the world's oldest national park?

Answer: Yellowstone National Park, which includes some of Montana, is the oldest national park. It was created by the United States congress and President Ulysses S. Grant on March 1, 1872.

3

TRUE OR FALSE:

Lewis and Clark visited the caverns that bear their name.

Answer: False. They passed below the entrance of the caverns but never realized they were passing a natural wonder.

4

What chilly event occured in Browning on January 23, 1916?

Answer: The world's greatest temperature change in 24 hours occurred on that day. The temperature in Browning dropped exactly 100 degrees.

5

There are many bears in Montana. What should you do if you bump into one?

Answer: Don't run away, just move back very slowly with your head tilted toward the ground. To avoid running into a bear in the first place, wear bells or make plenty of noise.

6

From December 1995 to May 1999, what speed limit was posted on Montana's major highways?

Answer: Montana pulled down its speed limit signs, replacing them with the sign "Reasonable and Prudent." This meant that it was up to individual drivers to choose a speed while traveling on Montana's highways. The state brought back speed limits after an increase in traffic accidents.

7

What happened to Montana's Grinnel Glacier in 1980?

Answer: When Mount St. Helens erupted in Washington in 1980, ash floated all the way to Montana. It covered the Grinnel Glacier. The dark ash kept heat in, instead of reflecting it as ice does. This caused an increase in the glacier's melting rate.

8

How did the Montana town of Ekalaka earn the nickname "Skeleton Flats"?

Answer: So many dinosaur bones have been found in Ekalaka that the town received this spooky nickname.

FOR MORE INFORMATION

Books

Markert, Jenny. *Glacier National Park*. Chicago: The Child's World Inc., 1993.

Pringle, Laurence. *Fire in the Forest: A Cycle of Growth and Renewal.* New York: Atheneum Books for Young Readers, 1995.

Schanzer, Rosalyn. *How We Crossed the West: The Adventures of Lewis & Clark.* Washington, D.C.: National Geographic Society, 1997.

Web sites

You can also go online and have a look at the following Web sites:

Montanakids.com
http://kids.state.mt.us

Lewis and Clark in Montana
http://lewisandclark.state.mt.us

A Carousel for Missoula
http://www.carrousel.com

50 States: Montana
http://www.50states.com/facts/mont.htm

Some Web sites stay current longer than others. Use your favorite search engine to find more about this state by entering keywords such as "Montana," "Rocky Mountains," "Billings," or any other topic you want to research.

GLOSSARY

chinook: a warm wind that blows from the mountains

distinguishes: identifies one kind from another

ecosystem: all living parts of an environment

environmentalist: a person who protects and cares for the environment

expedition: a journey made for exploration

extinction: when a species no longer exists

extraction: something that is obtained through a chemical process

gross state product: the annual total value of all goods and services in a state

metropolitan: a city with a population of 50,000 people or more

migrate: to move to a new place

moccasins: A shoe made entirely of soft leather, first worn by Native Americans

necessities: requirements for life, such as food, clothing, and shelter

powwow: a Native-American ceremony

reintroduce: to bring into an area after an absence

reservations: lands reserved for Native Americans

suffragette: a person who believes that women should have the same rights as men, such as the right to vote in elections

Superfund: the Environmental Protection Agency's fund that aids cleanup of environmentally unsafe or toxic areas

INDEX